Published in 2014 by The Rosen Publishing Group, Inc.
29 East 21st Street, New York, NY 10010

Adaptations to North American Edition © 2014 by The Rosen Publishing Group, Inc.
Copyright © 2014 Axis Books Limited

First Edition

US Editor: Joshua Shadowens

Library of Congress Cataloging-in-Publication Data

Bolitho, Mark.
 Fold your own origami army / by Mark Bolitho. — First edition.
     pages cm. — (Origami army)
 Includes index.
 ISBN 978-1-4777-1317-4 (library binding) — ISBN 978-1-4777-1465-2 (paperback) —
 ISBN 978-1-4777-1466-9 (6-pack)
 1. Origami—Juvenile literature. 2. Military miniatures—Juvenile literature. 3. Armies—Miscellanea—Juvenile literature. I.
Title.
 TT872.5.B65 2014
 736'.982—dc23
                                        2013005111

Manufactured in the United States of America

CPSIA Compliance Information: Batch #S13PK8: For Further Information contact Rosen Publishing, New York, New York at 1-800-237-9932

Origami
ARMY

Fold Your Own ORIGAMI
ARMY

Mark Bolitho

PowerKiDS
press
New York

CONTENTS

INTRODUCTION

You can use the ancient art form of **origami** to create some fantastic paper **tanks**, tents, and army officers. Origami has been a popular activity for centuries in Japan. The name origami comes from the Japanese words *ori*, which means "folding," and *kami*, which means "paper."

The US Army is the largest and oldest branch of the US military. The army protects the US and other countries on land. The army operates in more than 50 countries around the world. The army traces its origins back to the **American Revolution** when the **Continental Army** was formed on June 14, 1775. Over one million people work for the US Army.

The army's soldiers are divided into ranks from private to general. Ranks are used to determine status and responsibility. The higher ranks are called officers. Officers have authority over ranks lower than their own. In this book, you will learn how to create an army officer that will be at your command.

You will begin by learning basic **techniques**. Then, step-by-step instructions will help you make a variety of origami models. So start folding and creasing, and soon you will have your own origami army!

MATERIALS AND EQUIPMENT

All the projects in this book are made from square or rectangular pieces of paper. Here are the basic **tools** you need, and instructions for getting your paper to the right **proportions**.

All you really need is a pair of hands and a piece of paper. To achieve the best results keeps your hands clean, and use your fingers to manipulate the paper: enhance the creases using fingertips and nails.

CHOPSTICKS
A chopstick can be very useful for manipulating the inside of a model, particularly to work on the detail and create points.

RULER
You can use different tools to help you fold and to make sure your proportions are accurate. You can use a ruler to create straight folds and to sharpen creases.

SCISSORS
A good, sharp pair of scissors is invaluable for cutting paper. The best for the task have long, straight cutting blades.

MAKING A SQUARE FROM A RECTANGLE

Always start with a true rectangle—all four corners must be 90 degrees.

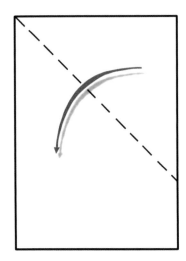

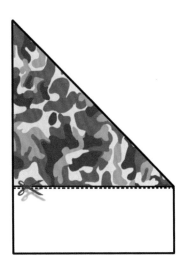

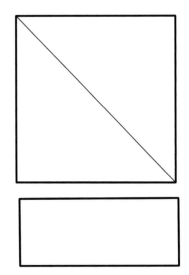

1 Fold the top edge of the paper diagonally so that the top edge aligns with the left-hand edge.

2 Fold the bottom edge of the paper up to the base of the triangle you have just made. Cut along this folded edge.

3 Unfold the triangle and the square is ready for use. You will have a square and a residual rectangle of paper.

MAKING A RECTANGLE FROM A SQUARE

Origami rectangles need to be of "A" proportions—A4, A3, A2. These stages show you how to get a rectangle of the correct proportions very simply from a sheet of square paper.

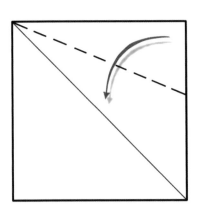

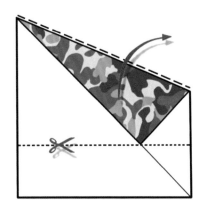

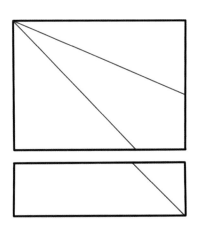

1 Fold the square in half diagonally and unfold. Now fold the top edge of your square so that it aligns with the diagonal crease.

2 Fold the lower edge of the paper up to the point at which the corner touches the diagonal crease. Cut along this crease.

3 Unfold the paper and a rectangle of the "A" proportions is ready for use. You will also have a residual rectangle.

9

BASIC TECHNIQUES

Although folding paper might seem the easiest of crafts, there are a few basic techniques to master before you can start. The construction process for each of the models in this book is illustrated using step diagrams. Alongside the diagrams you will find arrows and fold lines that show how a particular fold should be carried out. These are all explained on the following pages.

SYMBOLS

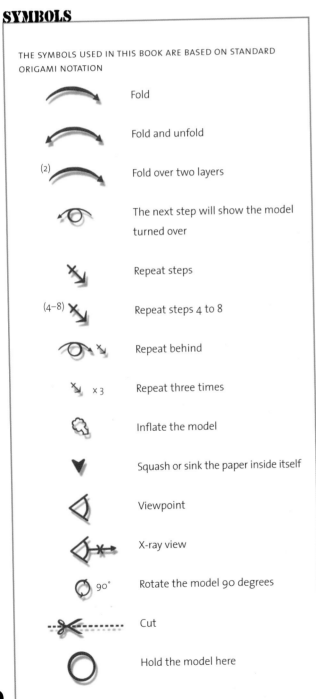

THE SYMBOLS USED IN THIS BOOK ARE BASED ON STANDARD ORIGAMI NOTATION

Fold

Fold and unfold

(2)   Fold over two layers

The next step will show the model turned over

Repeat steps

(4–8)   Repeat steps 4 to 8

Repeat behind

x 3   Repeat three times

Inflate the model

Squash or sink the paper inside itself

Viewpoint

X-ray view

90°   Rotate the model 90 degrees

Cut

Hold the model here

BASIC FOLDS

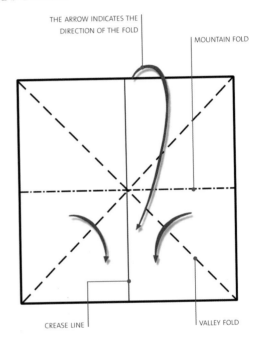

THE ARROW INDICATES THE DIRECTION OF THE FOLD

MOUNTAIN FOLD

CREASE LINE

VALLEY FOLD

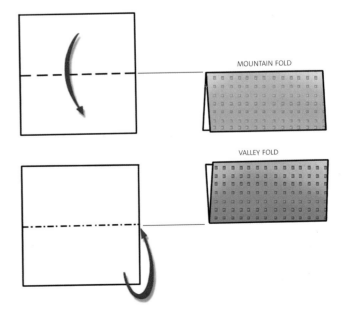

MOUNTAIN FOLD

VALLEY FOLD

FOLLOWING INSTRUCTIONS

The projects are broken down into a series of simple steps. Each step has a corresponding diagram that shows you how to make that step's folds.

Before attempting a step make sure that the model you have resembles the step diagram. Each diagram shows where to make each fold. The red arrows show the direction of the fold.

When you have completed a step, carefully look at the model to see if it resembles the next step. If your model does not look right, don't worry, just look closely at the instructions and try working back until you can match your model with an earlier step.

FOLDING TIPS

1	Follow the steps in numerical order, and fold one step at a time.
2	Look out for the reference points, both in the step you are trying to complete, but also by looking forward to see how the model should look when the fold is completed.
3	Fold as accurately as possible. If the step requires the model to be folded in half, fold and match the two edges of the model together and then make the crease.
4	You should fold on a flat, level surface. You can fold in the air, but it is easier to make clean accurate folds when working on a flat surface.
5	Make creases as sharply as possible. It may help to enhance the creases by running a fingernail or other object, such as a bone folder, along the folded edge.

FOLDING IN HALF

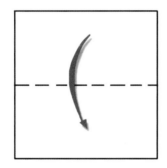

1 This diagram indicates that the square of paper should be folded in half.

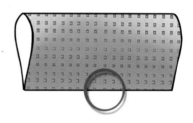

2 First of all line up the opposite edges and hold them together.

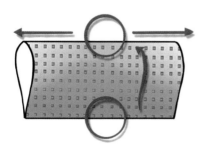

3 Now pinch at the center of the folded edge and make the crease, smoothing from the center out to the edges.

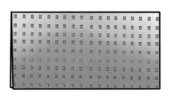

4 Keep holding the edges together as you sharpen the crease, the paper is now folded in half.

BASIC TECHNIQUES CONTINUED

REVERSE FOLD

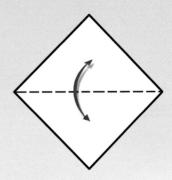

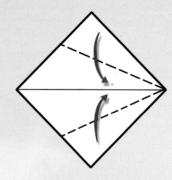

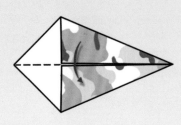

1 Fold and unfold the square of paper diagonally.

2 Fold the edges to the middle crease of the paper as shown.

3 Fold the model horizontally, along the middle.

4 This arrow indicates a reverse fold, along the dotted line.

5 This interim stage shows the point reversing into itself.

6 The reverse fold is now complete.

PRELIMINARY BASE

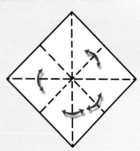

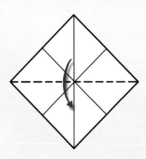

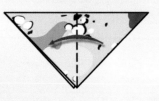

1 Fold and unfold the square in half horizontally, vertically, and diagonally.

2 Fold the square in half along one of the diagonal creases.

3 Fold in half again, along the center fold.

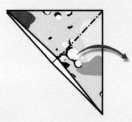

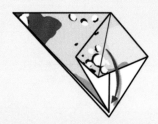

12 *4* Slip a finger inside the top layer and lift the paper.

5 Squash the paper down to flatten the point.

6 Turn over and repeat steps 3 to 5. The preliminary base.

WATERBOMB BASE

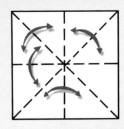

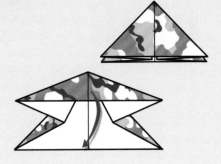

1 Fold and unfold the square in half horizontally, vertically, and diagonally.

2 Fold the square in half horizontally and reverse the folds in the diagonal creases.

3 Continue to fold and flatten the model, and it is complete.

BIRD BASE

Start with the completed preliminary base on page 12.

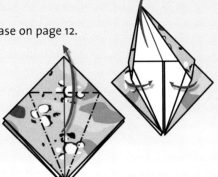

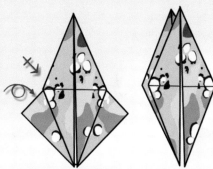

1 Fold and unfold the side edges and top corner, as shown.

2 Lift up the front layer and fold along the top crease. Fold in each of the sides.

3 Turn over and repeat steps 1 and 2 on the other side. The bird base is now complete.

FROG BASE

Start with the preliminary base on page 12.

1 Fold and unfold the side edge to the center crease.

2 Open the corner and flatten the paper along the new fold.

3 Fold and unfold the lower edges to the center crease.

4 Push the center section up and back. Refold the lower edges.

5 Repeat steps 1 to 4 on the other three points.

6 The frog base is complete and should look like this. **13**

TANK

This is a great project and real fun to make. It's in two parts so make the body of the tank before constructing the turret section.

PART 1: TANK BODY

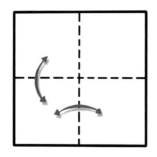

1 Pattern-side down, fold and unfold a square in half vertically and horizontally.

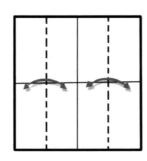

2 Fold and unfold the outer edges to the center.

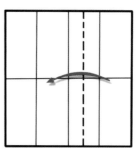

3 Fold over the right-hand edge so that the right edge touches the quarter line crease.

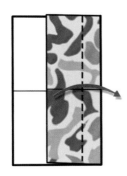

4 Fold the edge back to the right along the quarter line.

3-4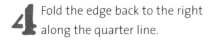

5 Repeat steps 3 to 4 on the left side of the model.

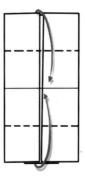

6 Now fold the top and bottom edges in to the middle crease.

7 Fold in all four corners to the folded edge, as shown.

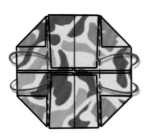

8 Fold the outer edges in to the center. Tuck them into the pockets in the center section.

9 Now fold and unfold the top and bottom edges.

10 Fold and unfold the outer edges to the quarter creases. Rotate the model 90°.

11 Gently blow into the aperture to partially inflate the base.

12 This section is now complete, put to one side.

THE TURRET

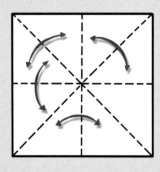

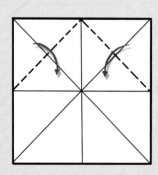

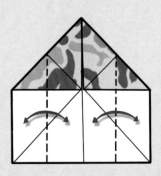

1 Pattern-side down, fold and unfold the square in half vertically, horizontally, and diagonally.

2 Fold the top two corners in to the center.

3 Fold and unfold the outer edges to the center crease.

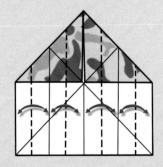

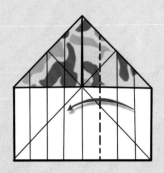

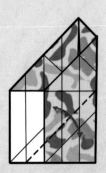

4 Fold and unfold between the creases already made, to divide the model into eighths.

5 Fold over the right-hand edge at the three-eighths line.

6 Fold and unfold the bottom right-hand corner diagonally, to the 1/8th crease as shown.

16

7 Reverse-fold the corner in to the model along the crease made in step 6.

8 Turn the model over to work on the other side.

9 Fold over the center line at on of the ⅛th creases. This will cause the second diagonal fold.

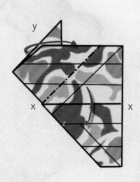

10 Fold over at x, while holding the lower section still. This will cause the fold at y.

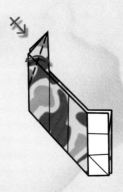

11 Fold and unfold the tip diagonally. Repeat this behind.

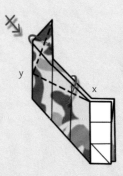

12 Fold over the front layer between x and y, this causes the paper to reverse the crease made in step 11. Repeat behind.

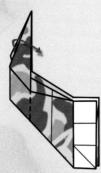

13 Fold the front edge over as indicated by the arrow.

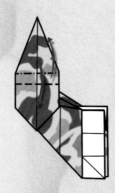

14 Fold the top point over and then back again.

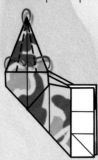

15 Fold the egdes of the top point to the middle and the tip over to blunt the gun barrel.

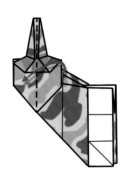 **16** Carefully fold the left section back together.

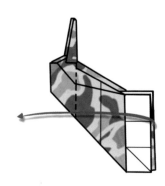 **17** Fold the top layer over. This will cause the layer beneath to open out. Flatten the model.

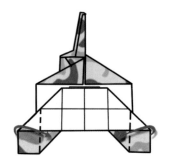 **18** Fold both outer edges over as indicated.

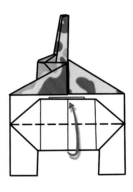 **19** Now carefully fold the bottom edge up.

 **20** Fold and unfold the outer edges to the middle.

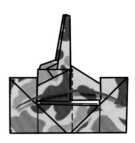 **21** Fold the model in half and rotate it 90 degrees.

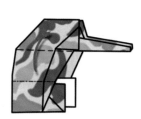 **22** Fold and unfold the edge up and back again. Repeat on the other side.

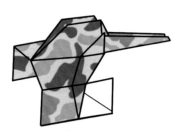 **23** The turret is now finished, and ready to attach to the tank base.

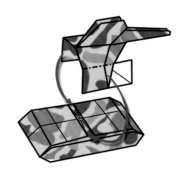 **24** Tuck the edges of the turret into the pockets in the base, the tank is complete.

TENT

You need **nimble** fingers for this one. Make sure you get it finished before it is time to make camp.

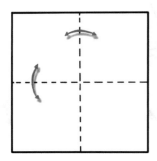 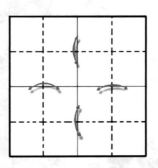 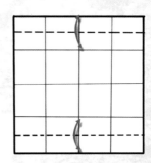

1 Pattern-side down, fold and unfold the square in half vertically and horizontally.

2 Fold and unfold the four sides to the center line, as shown.

3 Fold and unfold the top and bottom edges to the quarter creases.

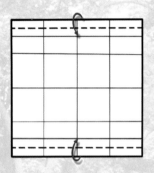

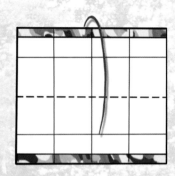

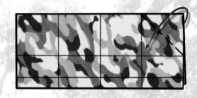

4 Fold the same two edges to the eighth creases that you made in step 3.

5 As neatly as possible, carefully fold the model in half.

6 Fold over the right-hand top corner, to the quarter crease made in step 2, as shown.

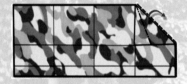

7 Raise the corner and carefully squash it flat.

8 Crease the bottom edges of the flattened section by folding and unfolding them.

9 Use your finger gently to lift the flattened section, as shown. Push it up and back. Now squash, refolding the folds made in step 8.

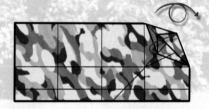

10 Lift the bottom right-hand corner and align the right side edge with the top edge of the model. This will make the diagonal fold shown above.

11 Make a second diagonal fold between the two creases.

12 Fold the squashed sections in half and turn the model over.

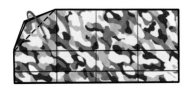 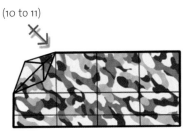 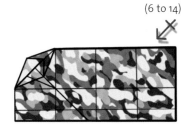

13 Fold the top left corner of the model over.

(10 to 11)

14 Repeat steps 10 to 11 on the left side.

(6 to 14)

15 Now repeat steps 6 to 14 on the right side.

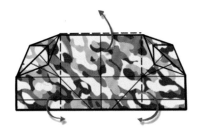 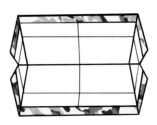 

16 Refold the original horizontal creases to form the shape of the tent.

17 This step shows the underside of the model, the next step will show a side view.

18 Refold the crease made in steps 10 to 11 to shape the tent.

19 Fold the small triangle down to connect the layers together. Repeat behind.

ARTILLERY

Take aim with this great-looking artillery piece. Heavy-duty weapons like this are indispensable in the field.

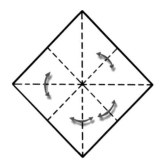

1 Fold and unfold the square in half vertically, horizontally, and diagonally, as shown.

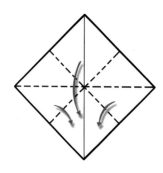

2 Fold the square in half along a diagonal fold, while doing this reverse the diagonal folds.

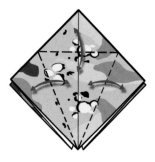

3 Fold and unfold the edges of the the model to the middle crease.

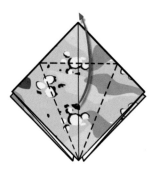

4 Lift up the front flap along the top crease, push it up and flatten. This fold will cause the folds made in step 3 to reverse.

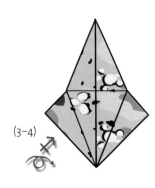

(3–4)

5 Turn over and repeat steps 3 to 4 behind.

6 Fold the bottom right-hand point up so that the left edge aligns with the model's center line.

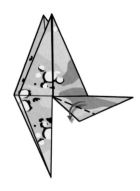

7 Fold the long edge of the point to align with the fold made in step 6.

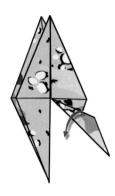

8 Now unfold the folds made in steps 6 and 7.

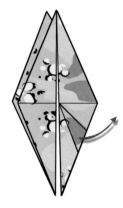

9 Now reverse the fold that was made in step 6.

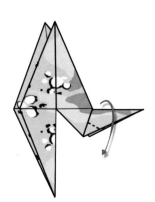

10 Next, reverse the fold that was made in step 7.

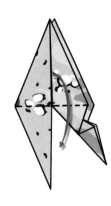

11 Fold the top point over the middle line to the front and rear.

12 Fold the left-hand edge of the model to the right, reverse-folding the point as you do.

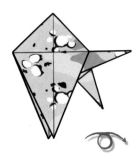

13 Turn the model over to work on the reverse.

14 Repeat step 12, working from right to left. Rotate the model 90 degrees.

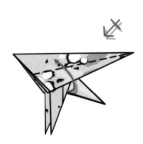

15 Fold up the front layer. This will cause a fold in the layer beneath. Repeat behind.

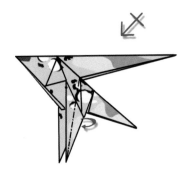

16 Fold the edge of the front layer of the leg into the model, as shown. Repeat behind.

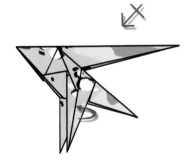

17 Fold the paper forming the leg into the model, as shown. Repeat behind.

18 Fold the edge of the middle leg behind and into the model, as shown. Repeat behind.

23

ARTILLERY CONTINUED

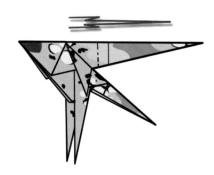

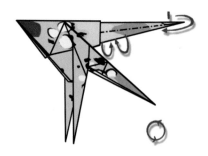

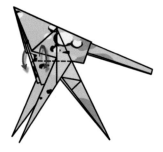

19 Reverse-fold the pointed end into and out of the model.

20 Narrow the gun barrel, and fold in the tip, and rotate the model slightly.

21 Hold the gun and fold the left side down into the model, causing the gun to rise.

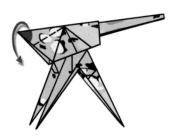

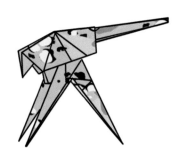

22 Make a reverse fold at the rear of the gun, as shown.

23 The artillery piece is now complete.

MEDALS

At the end of any military campaign you will need medals for your hard-working heroes. Here are some variations.

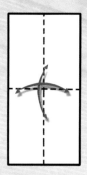

1 Pattern-side down, fold and unfold a rectangle vertically and horizontally.

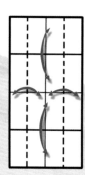

2 Fold and unfold each edge to the center of the rectangle.

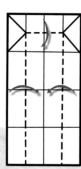

3 Fold the top edge to the quarter line. Fold in the outer edges and squash the corners flat.

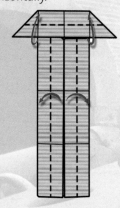

4 Fold the top edge up, this will cause the sides to open out and fold back on themselves.

5 Fold and unfold the model in half horizontally and diagonally between the two creases.

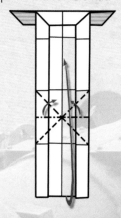

6 Fold the lower section up and reverse the diagonal folds.

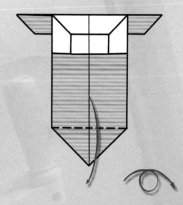

7 Fold the same section back down and turn the model over.

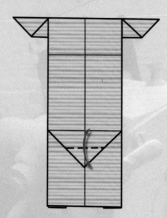

8 Fold and unfold along the middle of the triangle.

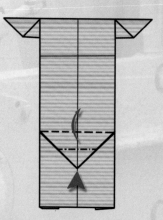

9 Fold one layer of the triangle up, this will cause the point to flatten. Squash it flat.

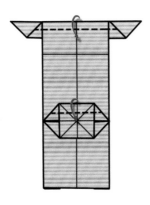

10 Fold over the two edges indicated.

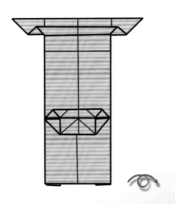

11 Now turn the model over and work on the other side.

12 Fold the top corners into the model.

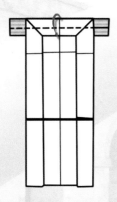

13 Fold the top edge of the model over.

14 Fold the corners of the lower section to the middle

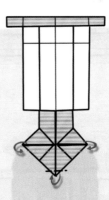

15 Now fold over the corners of the lower section to shape the medal.

STAR VARIATION

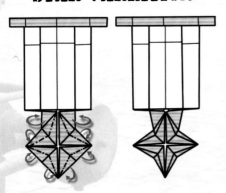

16 Start with step 15, shape the medal with reverse folds.

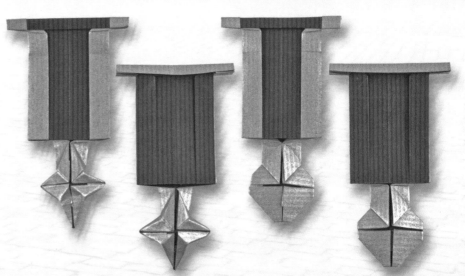

ARMY OFFICER

Officers hold a position of authority. This army officer can move his arms to give several different commands.

1 Pattern-side up, fold and unfold a square in half vertically, horizontally, and diagonally.

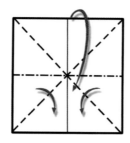

2 Turn the paper over. Fold the square in half horizontally and reverse the diagonal folds.

3 Fold and unfold the front flap on the right side to the meet the center crease.

4 Fold and unfold the crease made in step 3 to the middle.

5 Fold and unfold the crease made in step 4 to the middle.

6 Fold and unfold perpendicular to the crease made in step 5.

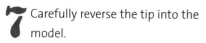

7 Carefully reverse the tip into the model.

8 Now turn the model over, to start on the other side.

9 As accurately as possible, fold the top flap down.

28

10 Fold the edges of just the top layer into the model.

11 Fold and unfold the bottom corners of the front layer.

12 Now fold up the front layer. This will cause the folds made in step 11 to reverse.

13 Fold and unfold the front layer diagonally, as shown.

14 Fold the front layer up, beneath the model, reversing the folds made in step 13.

15 Now you are ready to turn the model over.

16 Fold in the outer edges to align with the center crease.

17 Fold the top section down and back again.

18 Now fold the edges in either side of the head.

19 Reverse fold the bottom corners into the model.

20 Now fold the edges into the model.

21 Turn the model over to work on the other side.

22 Fold the edges in again either side of the model.

23 Fold the arms down to complete the model.

24 The arms can be folded to many different positions.

GLOSSARY

American Revolution (uh-MER-uh-ken reh-vuh-LOO-shun) Battles that soldiers from the colonies fought against Britain for freedom, from 1775 to 1783.

Continental army (kon-tuh-NEN-tul AR-mee) The army of patriots created in 1775 with George Washington as its commander in chief.

nimble (NIM-bul) Quick when moving.

origami (or-uh-GAH-mee) The art of folding paper into decorative shapes or objects.

proportions (pruh-POR-shunz) Proper or equal shares.

tanks (TANGKS) Military automobiles with heavy guns.

techniques (tek-NEEKZ) Methods or ways of bringing about a desired result in a science, an art, a sport, or a profession.

tools (TOOLZ) Objects that are specially made to help people do work.

FURTHER READING

Braulick, Carrie A. *U.S. Army Tanks*. Military Vehicles. Mankato, MN: Capstone Press, 2006.

Cooke, Tim. *US Army Rangers*. Ultimate Special Forces. New York: PowerKids Press, 2012.

Harasymiw, Mark *A. Army*. US Military Forces. New York: Gareth Stevens Learning Library, 2011.

INDEX

WEBSITES

Due to the changing nature of Internet links, PowerKids Press has developed an online list of websites related to the subject of this book. This site is updated regularly. Please use this link to access the list:
www.powerkids.com/orar/army/